POETRY
Aphorisms and Thoughts
By

TJ Ginn

Plea to Commune

Freedom shall not be limited though our vessel is very small. I yield my own direction when I hear my captain call. Our voyage is in peril our rations do deplete. All sailors to position, all maids to mend the sheets.

Our captain's course is frugal, true winds they shall prevail. All joined to answer muster our mission will not fail. Rejoice you maids of sailors, ships bellies full of meat. We tallied all together and the bounty we will eat.

Copyright © 2017 all rights reserved
Edit Release Sept 2019

Visit www.tjginn.com

About the Author

TJ is an electrical engineer who midlife sold out and started an organic farm. After five years and failing miserably with lots of excuses why, he returned in a fashion to electronics to aid in the development of eco-software as it relates to horticulture and land management.

Because of his love of horticulture, he became a self-studied horticulturalist and activist in developing growing techniques and involved himself in many areas of eco science, alternative energy and waste management.

Other Works
Available on Amazon.com and Createspace.com

The Ecstasy of my Dream
"A look inside the esoteric world that resides within you, how to reach it and what to do when you get there."

Children of the Seven Hills
Is it fiction or is it reality? This is a mind-blowing walk through how we got to where we are today. It is a fiction drawn from reality with so many, many things from our history that you will remember and can relate to. It explains philosophy and ideology and how it is we got to the zeitgeist of the day. This could be the unexpected awakening you were looking for.

Dilation - A science fiction that brings out the 'Buck Rogers' in all of us. It poses your most personal questions about space and time.

For the Love of Annie Dupree – A historical fiction about a young debutants adventure of traveling to Paris to study acting and discovering women's suffrage during the 1890's. Love and romance and the troubles found during this difficult age are hers to live and cherish

Table of Contents

4

Introduction

One can be stifled and intimidated by the magnanimous mind and never feel accomplished enough to express themselves.

That is the design of the 'Masters of the Glass Bead Game' who at the pinnacle of their narcissism are found hanging another piece of paper on the wall to award their accomplishment. One might remember Herman Hess.

I do not disrespect certification but only dream of a world where licensing did not equate to a right to life or opportunity. I only dream to be free from corruption, nepotism, and the clandestine passage of rights granted to the privileged.

You cannot learn enough, study enough, work enough or try hard enough to avoid the next critic lurking to prove you unworthy.

Critics are as numerous as roaches in garbage.

Just get rid of the garbage and your metaphysical solipsism is complete. It is not enough that Vincent van Gogh was ridiculed by the contemporaries and is quoted to say, "I wish they would only take me as I am." People even to this day must comment on his work rather than just look at it and with the greatest respect and say nothing.

Poems
From T J GINN's Blog –
T J GINN'S WRITERS BLOCK

Air

Consider the air, the substance, the thing we know so well but never see.

Air rushes through our fingers and blusters in our hair; it is soft, just soft as soft can only be.

Upon the air rides the fragrance of floral seduction that bees cannot resist, nor hummingbirds, nor butterfly nor me.

When speeding to the lungs air signals a gasp, desperate breath; could be fright; could be delight; that gasp before ecstasy.

The air welled up by the heat of a day blows ships, pushes waves, makes storms and takes lives.

The air pumped up fills balloons, whistles tunes, and at times puts rings around moons.

It's just air, never seen, always there, always there, thanks be, always there.

But just yesterday I saw the air. This thing you cannot see.

You were walking toward me and your dress and your hair were swimming. You were the breeze. You were the soft breeze. It could not be separated from you. It could not be separated from you. The air; you were the air don't you see? Don't you see?

And with my eyes I breathed you in. I breathed you in.

My Pensive Rain

On this day I woke to decide a necessary change, a welcome change, a relief.

Gray skies and cool morning dew foretell of light rain, a welcome rain; a rain that is due.

Clouds shroud the earth and make the world go away, leaves glisten with a spattering sound.

The agenda of tasks gives way, no work will be done today, no work on this day.

I can hear birds bustle to rest in the trees away from this welcome rain and the leaves glisten with a spattering sound.

A breeze now and then brushes past my soul and I feel rest, no tasks just rest.

Subtly a sadness is present, just there, not deep but there none the less; none the less it is there.

Is this lovely rain sad? Is this welcome rain a rain of sorrow, a weeping rain, a needed weeping rain?

Washing clean the forest, rinsing down the dust, quenching all the thirst, this rain, this pensive rain, this weeping pensive rain; this needed weeping pensive rain.

A time of sorrow, this time of sorrow, your time of sorrow will pass, it will pass but for now my love let it rain. Your tears let it rain, this beautiful cleansing pensive rain that glistens on the leaves with a spattering sound, a weeping sound, a restful sound this rain, this pensive rain.

The Anvil

This thing is a block of iron hammered to a tapered point on one end. It is bolted to a wooden stump to place it at a working height so the black smith or smithy can place glowing hunks of iron upon it to pound and shape the metal to something useful.

Fashioned are hammers, saws, shovels, plows; nails and screws and rings and chains.

Iron is a most malleable metal when heated and crushingly powerful when drawn into cold hard steel.

Its strength builds skyscrapers and bridges and ships the size of cities. Its forms are infinite and its compounds blend even to such a necessity that our own blood is red because of it.

Formed into a triangle and hung on a string it rings with a resonance that only it can produce, but the sound I am most consumed by is the sound of a hammer driving down to collide with the anvil.

This clank, driving clank of metal to metal is haunting me now.

I want to be the hammer. I want to pound. I want to drive the metal into a shape that I desire and can use, I want. I need. But when I swing the hammer, I can't find the anvil. Like swinging in the dark with zeal and missing. No anvil to connect with. The hammer in its ark continues down only to find my shin and in agony I yell, then fall to the ground and cry in disgust till the pain subsides.

I want to hear the clank of the hammer against the anvil because it is my desire to form the metal, I must form the metal; I must.

I'm hammering and in reality, I'm hammering this life, to form it into what I want but my hammer only strikes air leaving me broken at the shin. What else can I do but try again; so, I will. I will try again. One day I may hear the clank of my hammer striking the anvil and my life may become what I want you see; my life might become what I want; for what I want is you.

Appreciation

My need to be appreciated is a reflection of my compensation.
My annual taxation reflects the state of my usurpation.
My want to be respected is my daily occupation.
My daily need for bread is my contemplation.
My work of paltry need is my meditation.
My sadness of state needs remediation.
My anger at God is near to completion.
My contempt of you needs propitiation.
My suffering's complete in humiliation.
My lifting up of spirit is such jubilation.
My quandary was my thinking, my need for exaltation.
My need to be the answer as a renowned emeritus of recognition.
My want now only this, home and bread and time enough to show my
appreciation.

Excerpts from - "The Ecstasy of my Dream"

I Dream of You

I stood up in my little boat and gazed a mile to shore. No paper in hand and still I wrote a song and little score.

Calm seas and peace surround my way; sun setting on the main. I raise my arm to wave to her on land and in the sane.

I won't be long my nets are full I hail to her in song. I hoist the sail and make the turn; the day has been so long.

Pulling tight the sail to heal and tack I race my boat to shore. Your loving face and warm embrace a thing I so adore.

I'm dreaming verse and words so sweet, to tell you of my heart. The breaking waves on rocky reef my boat she broke apart. Ω

I would survive but the image of you faded and I awoke from a dream a sad but lovely dream. I knew her, I loved her but she was just a dream.

War Toys

I loved the toys for little boys; with nuts and bolts and grit. It was the age of wonder toys; with guts and jolts and spit.

Our tanks and guns they all made noise; and bombs with targets to hit. We killed the Germans with our toys; while the Nazi's got a writ.

You have no right now to exist; world courts have deemed it so. We have now declared the peace and let the prisoners go.

Our children see the news reels and ravages of war. The allies brought the final blow to settle all the score. Ω

War Addict's

In the ground are roots and blubs that make my belly sick. Eat what mother gives you and I'll teach you a little trick.

Sweet and kind won't tease your mind, though they are fun to lick. Look out for the red ones; they'll hit you like a brick.

With herbs and potions your mind in motion life is such a thrill. The mystery unfolds as you are told to defend, we all must kill.

Your friends have found a hiding place inside a little pill. Months and years will pass away with your pain residing still.

The journey's long they sing a song and still my bellies sick. Eat what mother gives you now here's the little trick.

Taking pills to thrill your mind, leaves horrors that will stick. With lots of sorrows in your tomorrows and habits hard to kick.
Ω

Be Right, Be Free

Crystal colors, transparent rocks and sand that's emerald green. I see ships that float in skies on clouds of ruby sheen.

Space unfolds in darkest blue with stars that mark the way. With beings of beauty more than true than anyone could ever say.

Mountains high and valleys low no warriors in my dreams. I am the king and jester too; nothing is what it seems.

I'm strong and tall then weak and small whatever I want to be. I'm Captain Smith of a frigate ship now setting out to sea.

It is quite well to play this game with no malice of intent. I dream of worlds where none are harmed and no blood is ever spent.

I'll teach you how to dream this way; it's really what you need. To be a righteous person, in thought and word and deed. Ω

Must Awake

What is real and what is not is something I forgot. Could it be the world we see is something that it's not?

If I should die before I wake, I pray my soul for God take. For in the spin my comfort wins, by faith for realities sake.

I like that dreams are never real, because if you do mistake. A fall from Eifel towers, no bones or legs will break.

I had a dream that in a dream, I struggled to awake. It was a gruesome feeling, one I had to shake.

I lurched and turned and kicked and squirmed to make it back to real. And when I woke with gasp and choke, thinking God what is the deal.

I looked now for familiar ground, to gain my where with all. I looked and looked and all around, the dream is all I saw. Ω

Dear Friends in Dreams

Seven volumes I held clutched in my arms; the work of all my friends. Distinctive works with all their charms; for me to find good ends.

The art was fine the colors true with poetry by finished hands. I held it all and loved it dear these tales of distant lands.

We reconvened one evening night to talk about the works. We were dismayed all gone astray so long that failure lurks.

Time swallowed up our memory and it was gone. It was just gone. Oh, the lament. It was just a dream. Ω

Your Boudoir

Naked are you before me; no shame in your boudoir. Our bodies are nestled together in a scene from film noir.

Enticing is your skin, and the shape across your thigh. You breasts are most inviting and your whim is never shy.

You tease my nimble body; I stroke you from within. For in your little chamber nary was there ever sin.

I'm amazed how well you know me as your fingers tease and play. Your beauty overwhelms me as my breath you take away. Ω

Skyscrapers

So amazed with the things I see. I wonder all the time. Could my mind be pleasing me? I awake to the morning chime.

I saw a city and buildings tall, impossible at the base. The buildings all went around I saw, could this really be the case.

I walked to look and sure it was each structure had a wheel. With massive beams and lengthy reach all made of shining steel.

I asked someone if they could say why the buildings go around. He said there is a reason, it's really quite profound.

He said the people like them and they do it all for fun. For every window dweller gets to see the morning sun.

Rotating skyscrapers? Give me a break. Ω

Dancer

I had an idea for a poem; an old man in a rocking chair. I did not ever know him, this feeble old gray hair.

He rocked with a steady rhythm and raised his wooden leg. I wanted to get to know him, so his pardon I did beg.

I said that I have seen you, once up upon the stage. I saw you in the who's who, your story in news front page.

Aren't you that fancy dancer, out on the Broadway scene? Yes he said I'm Prancer, I use to be so keen.

I said you were the best you know; nodding yes he bounced his leg. I still perform a nightly show; can't you see my bouncing peg. Ω

Sighting

Starry night and wonders abound across my velvet sky.
Shooting stars make not a sound and on the ground I lie.

I see some things I can't explain with lights that gleam and
speed. Before I know they fill the sky with sights that beam
take heed.

It is a battle from beyond by worlds we do not know. The
fighting siege from here and gone the ships fly very low.

Their numbers are amazing, they fill the very sky. Without a
moment's notice, deep space they all did fly.

I could not tell the time you see, my feelings are a rush. I knew
this sighting was for me, I keep it all a hush.

They are the future of our world, not far in time or space.
They're angels in our time unfurled, warring for the human
race. Ω

From the Novel "Children of the Seven Hills"

This is a posy for your curiosity, a quip to quench your thirst, a symposium for Socratic honor to the God Eros. Perhaps the encomium belongs to Plato whose stewardship led to script. A script past down through ages, it leaves us not alone, in the contemplation of Eros and the mysteries of love.

Eros

Scarred and bruised and broken, youth leaves us all so vain, for love is truly fickle when beauty is on the wane. You never lose your wanton eyes and loving of the fair. You did not choose a lovers lies, nor the graying of your hair.

Seeking and learning and knowing, wise sayings from the past. Praises hale to our God Eros whose love eternal lasts. With beauty gone none ring your bell your time is all alone. A well springs forth and time will tell the magic you have sown.

A child came forth, a product of your youthful need to sire, a shallow love of visceral want and object of your desire. A passion not of first request with needs they do require, of spirit and reason and intellect of you they do inquire.

The bell rings a beautiful sound as you answer Eros' call. A love so strong came raining down bestowed upon us all. Agape love, a giving love, God Eros he had smiled, for there is no greater love, as a parent's for a child.

Malaise

Out of the darkness comes fear, the evil, the cold and the cruel. Eyes stare hard in the remembrance of sight but no light is at hand to see. A presence is sensed and quickly I turn to face the direction of my fear, but I am an entity without members, no limbs, no arms and no legs.

I exist for I am thinking and remembrance of tutor Descartes. What manor of being here am I. What mind, in what body do I think. No windows no doors, am I up, am I down, I dream a horrible dream, a dream whose end I beseech.

Be done with me, now you let me go, you dastardly cognition, you horrible clutch, you dark and fearful dream of the evil, the cold and the cruel. Stare hard, can you see, can you see stare hard, but no light is there, no light to see. There is no light for me.

Again, I feel a sense of fear, and turn with no limbs to see. Who is there, who is there, I think to yell but no mouth portends to speak? What am I, who am I, where am I, I think that I think to think.

Weeping ensues, or the remembrance of such, I would if I could have eyes. I thrash and I fight in thoughts I take flight or remembrance of such an act.

What am I, who am I, where am I, I dream that I think that I think to think.

The Well of Souls

The boy asked Merlin, "How deep is the well of souls?" Merlin replies,

Miles and piles of devils trials with Jupiter on the wane, I once began to count the stars, my efforts were all in vain.

I counseled Venus and then Mars their answers were the same, there's a hundred thousand million souls in every drop of rain.

Poems and Prose

Poem Noir

I dream in color and passion red with shadows of black and white.

It's a simple thing that marks my rise from films and histories fight.

It is not a pretty picture though they want to make it so.

The stories are the lecture, on the screens in theaters glow.

They shape the moral ideologue with judgment of the crime.

And we the jury of the dialogue, our opinion is valued prime.

Film noir is dark and brooding, with questions for us all.

It poses lusts and criminal goading, will our social temple fall.

What darkness lurks in the viewers mind as murderous scenes unfurl.

Do they find they are of the villain's kind as the hair begins to uncurl?

Or is rather a rapturous plot when the evil villain is caught?

And the lovers swoon in the evening moon with a moral lesson Taught. Ω

Film Noir has a vague definition. Is it a certain type of film that has a dark romanticism?
Look up the definition and you will find it means different things to different people.

The Adoration of Kindness

One might say that grace is the ultimate state of being rising above the noise of discontent. But then discontent stems from want, the want to be nourished, the want to be sheltered from the many harms of our physical existence.

Intelligence can artfully dance upon the sea of our material world. We ogle the masters of the 'Glass Bead Game' rendering our service to their wisdom and the very shares of our labor to buy the luxury that can distance us momentarily from our discontent.

Ideologically we way in the balance our governance of right and wrong and by discourse defend our means or wage or right to be. Under freedom and democratic argument, we determine our justification of the classes from poor to bourgeois to opulent or even megalomania.

One might consider that a beggar on the street that refuses to work, with the exception of mental illness, is a tyrant allowing your children to labor in their stead to provide for their needs and wants. Could this mean that charity in this case is miss-given? Thus, many pass by a vagabond with a sign, "Will Work for Food," unless they will really work for food. Some just succumb and think, "If you are so low that you need to be on the street with a sign, you are truly needy." They render up a bill or two and feel they have done charities' call.

So as you meander through this incomprehensible realm look deep into the eyes of your fellows, discerning each individual by the best of your judgment and render grace and kindness where it is due, even unto your adversary when found in need and he will no longer be your adversary.

Now the world is contrary to this with its brutal economic competition until there is devastation, then wonders never cease as the kind come forth to give all that they have.

We are at our best when we are broken and don't you adore when someone is kind.

For I was an hungered, and ye gave me meat: I was thirsty, and ye gave me drink: I was a stranger, and ye took me in: Naked, and ye clothed me: I was sick, and ye visited me: I was in prison, and ye came unto me.

Contrition

Contrition, contrite, repentance, remorse, regret, sorrow, sorry, penitent, apologetic.

Grace, forgiveness, elegance, refinement, loveliness, polish, beauty, poise, charm.

The order of terms suggests that you cannot have the latter without first being broken.

And thus the necessity of the differential, without it there is no meaning.

Ignorance proceeds wisdom and even God cannot prevent this existential truth.

We weep for our children knowing the path to knowledge is suffrage.

Would that you could tell them but they will not listen until burned.

The world is an incorrigible child not yet contrite. Oh the sorrow!

Evening

I whistled a little tune on the sunset of this day.
I whistled a little tune for my dreams had gone astray.
I whistled a little tune for my spirit was light and gay.
I whistled a little tune in the hopes that you would stay.

The light is slowly dimming and your face is slightly gray.
My love for you is brimming and I beg for you to play.
I know your songs and hymning, signs that you're going away.
This day I'm left foreboding, adieu the sun and crimson ray. Ω

Puerile

One is drawn to the base to gain definition, who am I, what am I, where am I and what is right and what is wrong or rather what can I do and what is contemptible.

Perhaps contemptible is too erudite for one must consider the differential.

You would do nothing unless you must.

What does this mean?

You would not get out of bed unless the coals on the fire were not warming you enough.

I do digress to an earlier age when one had to stoke the fire for warmth.

Misanthropic delusions of this age of ease, you merely turn up the thermostat on your gas fired furnace and digitally control your comfort.

What is worse is that you are too ignorant to understand how the computer integration of your digitally controlled thermostat works.

This is the isolation and separation. You do not understand your realm. You click and paste and play the surface of what is completely manipulated beneath you.

You have allowed it. It is increasing in complexity and no one is responsible.

Try and find someone who will take responsibility.

Come home and plant some seeds and grow real food. You can't eat a digital phone and video games get boring.

Your Garden

I am enjoying your garden and it causes me verse because I have not one of my own.

Don't you know that the best we can be is the labor of our own hand and this is lost?

True knowledge of the cultivar and the seed that springs forth is relegated to the dead.

I do not think it is intentional, this dumbing down of our species.

Our children have been coddled away through laziness and shiny toys.

They built the coliseum for gladiator games on the bones of ignorance.

I herald your garden and planting of seed and the treasure of the knowledge it expounds.

Simple times, simple people is not condescension, it is lament.

Let us be thankful that we knew them, these simple times, these simple people and me.

I would Rather

I would rather have fifteen years of calm than fifteen minutes of fame.

I would rather be an aged oak standing firm upon the ground than the rush of many saplings that are scattered all around.

I stand against the axmen with ambition to cut me down. He hacks against my sinew well knowing I am bound.

I would rather be a mockingbird dancing on the wing, for my stage is not ambition and I truly like to sing.

So there you have the might oak with a bird to dance its crown. Laughing at ambition for none could cut him down.

Savor the day and slow down. Life is long if you choose.

Collection of Thoughts

I became serious about being an author in 2008. Though I had authored many writings throughout my life, I never considered them literary works and never considered myself an author. I would suggest that you should teach your children early on that even if they think what they write at the time to be insignificant, their viewpoint may and probably will change. Moments of inspiration come at different times in a long life and if you write even one poem or posy or quip and even a story, you can consider yourself an author.

I use the analogy that if you have an opinion you are a philosopher; that if you speak a word you are an orator and if you think, your thoughts have important relevance to us your fellows. If you write them down there is a chance it will be here for posterity. If you do not they are forever lost.

The following is a collection of thoughts and expressions. I hope that they will be thought provoking or even you might find us kindred.

Hate

Misanthropic, Misogynistic and Misandry require contemplation even for the erudite elitist on a quest of intellectual pursuit to be sure that they were not deficient in their studies, for even they must pause.

Misanthropic is the hatred of humans of all ilk's, while Misogyny is the hatred of women and Misandry is the hatred of the male.

Consider self-loathing before any contemptuous considerations. In order to hate something, you must be something so all of these become self-loathing.

You animal. You defecator. You wash and polish your appearance with perfume to cover your inadequacy and then purport to express your disgust of the existence of others.

Loneliness is your prescription, isolation and separation till you cry for conversation.

And out of the darkness came want. The primal scream to be and not be alone.

And then you hate no one or anything and love is all that is.

Incomprehensible Beauty of the Differential

So, let us think about it in the simple physical realm.
Simple does not mean simplistic but rather not complex which
in itself is a differential.

The Cognitive simple physical differentiations by the animal species...

One should recognize that the animal species includes all
cellular incarnations from virus to complex protein manipulated
complexes. They are...

Light vs. Dark
Hard vs. Soft
Hot vs. Cold
Fast vs. Slow
Macro vs. Micro

The Complex metaphysical differentials by the animal species

One should note that the physical differentials do not exist
without the essential animal, i.e., 'the observer' who
existentially places the metaphysical differential realities
juxtaposed to raw matter physicality with its cognitive
interpretation.

Love vs. Hate
Joy vs. Grief
Fear vs. Fearless or Peace and Safety
Jealousy and/or vengefulness vs. Grace
Empathetic vs. Indifference
Right vs. Wrong
Just vs. Unjust or Righteous vs. Unrighteous

One could go on with other juxtapositions but in most cases, they would fit under one of the afore mentioned existential differentials.

I.E

Good vs. Bad
Compassionate vs. Uncompassionate
Proper vs. Improper
Kind vs. Unkind

Existential Theory / Philosophy

Deal with what is real!
Existential activism - recognize physical vs. metaphysical.

This is not in defense of irrational thinking and this is a rhetorical statement.

There is no separation from the physical and metaphysical.

There is no escape

YOU ARE WHAT IT IS, WHICH MEANS YOU ARE THE HUMAN BEING THAT EXISTS AND THAT UNLESS PHYSICAL LAW CHANGES YOU WANT THIS:

**LIFE
GOOD NOT BAD
RIGHT NOT WRONG
RATIONAL NOT IRRATIONAL
FAIR NOT UNJUST**

I would contend that if you do not want this you are dangerously outside the norm of human compassion or understanding.

THE POWER STRUGGLE IS INEVITABLE

As Fredrick Nietzsche described in his philosophy of "The will to Power"

ARISTOCRATIC MEGALOMANIA IS A HUMAN LUST

COMMUNISTIC FASCISM IS A NATURAL EXISTENTIAL RESPONSE

In that the ideology of communism is self-rule but the interim dictatorship required turned it into fascist absolute control. The ideology of communism is a defense response to an oligarchy of wealthy capitalists.

CHOSE COOPERATIVE EGALITARIAN SOCIETAL SENTIMENTALITY – IT IS A CHOICE NOT A DICTATE

This is best observed in American Democracy where capitalism and competition are balanced by communities coming together for common cause.

OR CHOSE NARCISSISM … AND UNBRIDLED WANT

You think it won't happen?

IT ALREADY HAS HAPPENED.
HATE KNOWS NO BOUNDS UNTIL ALL IS LOST
AND THE REMNANTS LEARN 'LOVE' FROM THE DEAD.

TAKING WITHOUT GIVING DRAINS US ALL.

THE MOST IMPORTANT DIFFERENTIAL

IGNORANCE vs. ENLIGHTENMENT

The most unavoidable differential…

"To be or not to be"

"You may not get this until you at deaths door."

So why wait, forgive and love someone NOW!
Before they are dead to tomorrow and the only tragedy is that…

'You are not listening and don't care'

The Oedipus Animal

Oedipus Greek: Οἰδίπους *Oidípous* meaning ("swollen foot") was a mythical Greek king of Thebes. He fulfilled a prophecy that said he would kill his father and marry his mother, and thus brought disaster on his city and family. This legend has been retold in many versions and was used by Sigmund Freud to name the Oedipus complex.

Human sexuality as proved is an amorphous existential observation of a true differential that plots on a hysteretic bell curve that plots to the natural logarithm of what is normal.

There is no possibility that you understood what I just said. So, look below.

Hermaphrodite
In biology, a **hermaphrodite** is an organism that has reproductive organs normally associated with both male and female sexes.

Homosexuality is romantic or sexual attraction or behavior between members of the same sex or gender. As a sexual orientation, homosexuality refers to "an enduring pattern of or disposition to experience sexual, affectionate, or romantic attractions" primarily or exclusively to people of the same sex.

Heterosexuality is romantic or sexual attraction or behavior between persons of opposite sex or gender in the gender binary. As a sexual orientation, heterosexuality refers to "an enduring pattern of or disposition to experience sexual, affectional, physical or romantic attractions to persons of the opposite sex."

This is a natural log rhythm of hysteresis which is an observed phenomenon derived from practical measurements and mathematical theory.

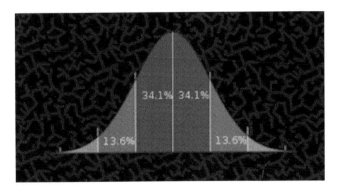

Statistically heterosexuals occupy the majority of the curve and hermaphrodites and homosexuals are on the outside of the curve. Thus, societal acceptance of sexual norms follows the indicated arithmetic if one considers majority statistics indicative and suggestive of what is normal.

Psychosexual infantilism - Psycho-logic defense – Dénouement by **Sigmund Freud** can be countered by mere simplicity of thought.

Children are effervescent and quiescently blind. They bloom from the darkness of a void of knowledge and become. They respond to their new body that responds to the differentials of hard, soft, light, dark, warm, cold and delight, pain. They cry when discontent and coo when happy.

Instinctually they respond to a physical compulsion of genital stimulation with no rationality and with no emotional connection except self-adulation and these are considered natural. It is no different than nursing on the breast. It involves no learned behavior or permission. It is pre-cognitive.

Procreation would not occur without fornication between male and female, except that in the modern scientific age this is no longer necessary. Now consider beyond the mathematical bell curve and consider sexuality beyond the purpose of procreation.

The Absurdity of the mechanism of the Orgasm.

Shrouded in the framework of the Human Psyche is a physiological point of ecstasy. Mysteriously planted in our realm and perhaps in the realm of all other species is a psychological / physiological juxtaposition called the orgasm? What does this mean?

Certain physical actions and stimulations and certain thoughts or mental excitations in the metaphysical (thought world) cognition (thinking) causes the orgasm. It requires mental arousal in image and imagination in conjunction with physical stimulation to produce the orgasm.

Children hide their Sexuality.

Instinctually children hide. How is it that they know, not shame but discernment of disclosing their titillation, their excitation and their naked exposure? They feel no quilt but hide their secret.

Brutalization by association.

If you are not like me you are not acceptable.

Again, the Existential Absurdity of the Orgasm.

Proved is the biochemical hormonal function of testosterone on the sexual libido of both male and female. Don't argue this, if you have doubt look it up.

And the King would allow only Eunuchs (castrated males) to serve the Queen.

You cannot describe color to the colorblind; nor sight to the unsighted, or even sound to the deaf, and no mortal can describe the compulsion for the orgasm and children hide their most secret discernment.

The only animal that wears clothes is the human animal. Prolific are the religious scriptures pertaining to nakedness and the insinuation of the shame of your nakedness.
Children as toddlers have no inclination of shame. Quickly, by their parent's instruction, they are taught to cover and thus we hide our most secret discernment.

And thus, we harbor our most critical judgment. Are you chaste (pure, innocent, uncorrupted, virtuous, honorable, and unsullied?)

One might consider that the circumcision of the male is the religious and furthermost extension of naked shame. It calls you to rise above your animal instinct, reconcile the compulsion of the orgasm with responsibility and think about the consequences of your actions. One might consider the Jewish law of circumcision on the eighth day. A child is given no choice, but it is done to them. You will know your shame and we have cut you a priori.

In Judaic Law only is the continuation of the circumcision by law, requiring chastity, condemning infidelity and extramarital fornication.

The Unbridled Libido

Hedonism suggests animal disregard. Fornicating without regard to the connection between the orgasm and procreation is pure animal ignorance. Humans without limits breed without limits and without limits in a finite resource such as the earth; the only control is the natural collapse of the system.

There is no defense against the all-powerful orgasm without law and education. You will have to watch the suffering on scales you cannot imagine.

The Oedipus Animal

Well known is the fact that the male animal sires such as cats and dogs, wolves and lions will kill the young males and eat them. It is assumed that they are eliminating their possible sexual competition. It would stand to reason that if a male animal survived thanks to its mother's protection, that he would be endeared to his mother and come into competition with his father; perhaps not over the mother alone, but for all the females. Existential scientific observation bears out this truth.

The Nurturing Father

Not uncommon in all species is the male that assumes the female role in nurturing the young, both male and female offspring; this is especially true in the human animal since there is no record of fathers killing sons for fear of competition. Placing the human male as a villain by generalization has no statistical foundation. It cannot even be placed on the bell curve

43

because factual documentation can find no incident of the *Oedipus Complex* in reality. It only exists in mythology. After adolescence the male is nurtured by the fathers adoration to guard and protect and instruct the male child as to the nature, strength and toughness that is extraordinarily required of him. These are isolation, suppression of weak emotions, endurance and competition. This is done by a nurturing father to build strength in his son for protection and confidence building.

Thus, the Oedipus Complex as to the male child in competition for the mothers affection should be laid to rest as a fallacy so rare that it cannot fit in to any statistical model.

Again, the Oedipus Animal

The world is in danger of overpopulation due only to the hormonal compulsion for the orgasm. Copulation as freewill renders us powerless. Rendering the female with unwanted child and worse of all, abandoned for she has no means to support the offspring.

The only peril

A society that cannot control blatant ignorant copulation and unbridled population growth will surely perish.

Simple Answer

Require Legitimacy and Responsibility.
Provide Free birth control
Provide Free Tubal Ligation's and Vasectomies.
Allow early intervention with RU486
Preserve a woman's choice.
Hold both parents accountable financially.
Teach abstinence, responsibility, love and respect for the child.

If you are looking for a point at which the soul enters the body, consider this from the Hebrew Genesis7 And the LORD God formed man of the dust of the ground, and breathed into his nostrils the breath of life; and man became a living soul.

One might consider that the first breath of the infant is the entry of the soul and it awakes to life and becomes an autonomous entity.

Rendering Compassion

Rendering Compassion; perhaps distilling your care.
How do I know if my concern has been usurped, am I a fool and when do I discern?

Mine own heart is stopped at this consideration by the very charge that is presented before us. In the tempest of destruction, whom do you chose to save? I choose all who cry out, and I reach out to raise them up in want of my very soul for I assume they are of kindred kind and I so wanted to save them, and then they devoured me in deception.

How can one discern? How can one know? Know only your honesty to yourself.

The Incredible Lightness of Being

Warning – Human angst is inconsolable.

Now, this may seem to be inspired by the film, "The Unbearable Lightness of Being," however this is not plagiarized. It rather is inspired by experience.

Never were there truer words that "Ignorance is Bliss," for it is this necessary requirement that compels adventure. Educated sages will contemplate at infinitum and never move where "Fools Rush In."

Impetuousness is the harbinger of the young, albeit misguided by the patriarchs and matriarchs that precede them. This includes the daunting task of the laws justification of what is right and what is wrong.

The prospect of setting right the wrong dumbfounds us all with the precept that we as simple finite little humans, and I emphasize 'little,' are not responsible, and thus is the human angst to surrender to that which is beyond their control. It is all too big for me.

We allow atrocities and dodge bullets hoping to be spared, knowing that our short life has little meaning, thus allowing megalomaniacs to lead the world to utter consumption and devastation. We are Lemmings on a course of destruction and cannot stop.

So *laissez-faire, que sera sera,* none of this is my fault.

Simple answer - Require legitimacy, stop the population, stay home and grow food.

Your ability to entertain your short little life is filled with bigger, better more. Star Trek is a fiction and while you are trying to get somewhere you cannot realize that you are already there. I'm not saying don't advance your knowledge and science but gain control of your lusts.

I would hope that you would realize this and stop milling around the world because you are only going in circles and do not realize the "Incredible Lightness of Being." But, you will not, and this is not my fault.

Grace

Existential solipsism to complete your narcissism is only accomplished in this contemporary age for a few moments until you are broken down on the highway with a flat tire and a homeless mechanic comes to your aid to loosen the bolt you could not. He changed your tire and sent you on your way and you gave him a twenty and said thanks.

Welcome to the future. Either you become cooperative or you perish. What does this mean?

Have <u>love one to the other</u> or perish. Everyone is ugly. Gain your beauty through grace.

Give it, love it, become it. The greatest of all the spirits or metaphysical implantations is Love, Hate, Joy, Grief, Fear, Jealousy and <u>Grace</u>. Be possessed by Grace. It is the best you can be.

Shiny Gifts

Shiny gifts of diamonds and gold and the lust to provide your heart throb with enticing magnetism to draw her to physically succumb and rend herself to your desires and notwithstanding the modern acceptance of cross gender indulgence, this has brought to mind...

Shaka ka Senzangakhona the Zulu chief conquered by the English in the 18th century made a political statement that astounded the English commanders and statesmen.

King Shaka of the Zulu

How do you catch a monkey? His response was "You put something shiny in a bottle." The monkey will reach to grab the shiny thing and grasp it tightly. The monkey so wants the shiny thing that it will not let go. It cannot run away with the weight of the bottle and it will not let go of its prize. You can then grab the monkey and roast it for dinner.

Never consider yourself to be more than a monkey chasing a shiny thing, an animal called to higher thought. Can you overcome? A diamond is just a rock and the monkey will give its life to have it.

Socialism in Other Words

Do your social studies homework and what you will find is ideology. It is the continual argument as to who has the right to life and by what means. Don't let anybody fool you that this is a complex subject. It is all about who owns what, who gets what and who the boss is. In the USA we have a bunch of lying thieves called the congress who dole out the goodies to their buddies and get paid to do it. It is complete hypocrisy with demagoguery playing on the ignorance of the people to sway votes to their side.

What is right? Less government, less rules, low taxes, conservative or more government, more rules, tax controls, liberal.

The communist model by Marx, Lenin, Trotsky and Stalin turned into a fascist dictatorship and it failed because without individual autonomy and private ownership, pride, ambition and property protection disappear. Communal property becomes dilapidated because no one cares about it.

The concept of communism came about because unbridled capitalism and its ambition to possess leave the proletariat working class people in poverty with municipalities devastated in waste. The wealthy entrepreneur with cash in hand moves away and lives elsewhere.

Our system in the USA attempts to balance the protection of the individual and the pride of ownership and not let the Capitalist run away with all the money leaving the working people that made them rich with nothing. There you have it. SOCIALISM. Our brand of socialism is the continual protection of the individual with freedom and opportunity and the law to prevent the wholesale rape by capitalists and take no responsibility for the community of the human race.

Everyone wants freedom, everyone deserves life and no one owns the natural resources and that includes oil and natural gas and the companies who use it should pay us for the privilege by fair pricing. Your cost of living is directly related to fuel costs and those prices are fixed by the oil barons that are nested together to keep prices high.

Angst

Existential theory goes like this… A man walks to the edge of a cliff and has fear that he could fall over the edge and die, but he then stops, meditates and thinks, what if I just throw myself over the edge. Thus, is your angst, the temptation and quizzical, personal challenge of your existential life or existence.

When you were a child and you approached the loose tooth in your jaw and you pondered pulling it out or not, you had 'angst.' While you took days pushing and pulling on the tooth or whether you pulled it out or not, is not a measure or your bravado, for in the sleep of death what dreams may come.

I am quoting Shakespeare's mortal coil. If you do not know what that means, try a Google search.

We are continually at the precipice of the best we can be and need not throw ourselves off the cliff to prove our sacrifice.

Megalomania is a disease as bad as cancer. It is okay to be simple. Stop the madness.

Societal despondence, your true Angst

You can't agree on anything. You don't like each other. You need to get away, but there is nowhere to go except out.

It is not your fault. There is something seriously wrong with human society. Can it be fixed?

The wilderness used to provide you with your escape where you could run and be wild with no law, but that is gone. You circle in on each other in your society and point and blame and imprison each other for your lack of your wild freedom and you do unjust entrapment and murder.

Your children are born to your disease of megalomania and oppression under the guise of your historical struggle for freedom when truly you are a carnivorous beast with no sense of the ideology that compels you. God save that you would have a brain to stop your lust.

Stop. Stop building, stop fornicating, stop illegitimacy of the child, stop gambling, stop lying, stop hating, stop being prideful, stop killing, and stop your wicked imaginations.

But I fear you are not smart enough to know the six, yea seven things that the Lord doth hate.

Can it be fixed? I fear not.

God wants you broken and dead

You are trying to fix what is broken. You are trying to solve the insolvable. You want life eternal but your logic and intellect fails and, in your angst, you blame God. Who else can you blame for your condition? It is certainly not your fault. No one asked you if you wanted to be born and all of this is certainly not your solipsism.

Yet you support and promote... What is it that you support and promote?

You support violence, you support megalomania, you support idolatry and icons, and you support the love of the rich and famous and a machine that cannot stop its blatant consumption of more and more want and the slaves that feed its needs.

Come home to real life. It is possible. Just start a garden, read a book and slow down. What you need is right out your back door in the dirt.

Your Love of Violence

Justifiable violence is the defense of life and limb from oppression. The civil war of the US, The Bolshevik revolution, WWI, WWII, The Korean conflict, Vietnam, the Contra war in Nicaragua, the coup of Pinochet in Chili and his prosecution for war crimes.

You may question many of these as you chose your side. Is it indignation that compels you to violent recourse? Sometimes, Perhaps, but are you justified?

You are a violent person. You get in your car and immediately you are a worrier flipping the finger at the oppressor who cut you off.

Just yesterday at the air show in Las Vegas Nevada a plane crashed and people were killed. They were just spectators but it was their love of violence that took them to the show. Think about it.

What you really want is the Roman Gladiators duel to the death. You condone it every day with your money and support.

You get what you deserve. "Thou shalt not tempt the lord thy God"

A violent world gets violence. What do you expect?

A Necessary Separation

Innocence is a necessary separation from the adult world. This is something that people understood years ago. That is why we have age separation with the age for a driver's license and the minimum age to drink. It is why we prevent minors from smoking which is the first vice they sneak.

You are not getting this... Children steal their _**sneak**_ into the adult world of corruption. Allow their brief freedom and hide your addiction to debauchery or perhaps clean up your act and become a good person.

Let children be children and grow up at their own pace without exposure to decadence.

Good Luck

Mark Twain and Huck Finn are waiting at the creek. Come home and stop the madness.

Contempt

Shakespeare invented his words and his poetry and prose and somehow it became law.
Cut and paste any of Shakespeare's works into a word processor and it is colored with errors and correction recommendations.

What I am saying to you goes like this…

Matthew 13:54
[54]And when he was come into his own country, he taught them in their synagogue, insomuch that they were astonished, and said, Whence hath this man this wisdom, and these mighty works?
[55]Is not this the carpenter's son? is not his mother called Mary? and his brethren, James, and Joses, and Simon, and Judas?
[56]And his sisters, are they not all with us? Whence then hath this man all these things?
[57]And they were offended in him. But Jesus said unto them, A prophet is not without honor, save in his own country, and in his own house.
[58]And he did not many mighty works there because of their unbelief.

I say…
How can this man be an Author, philosopher and theologian when I found a spelling mistake or a grammatical error? Self-publishing has allowed in the riffraff dogs. Disregard their thoughts or teachings, it is now a world less than the great ones left only to the mongrels.

And how can you be a painter Modigliani. Who gave you permission to be?

My contempt is reaching new horizons.

Modigliani a true master.

Don't

Don't think in finite terms.
Don't think that people do not change.
Don't think that governments cannot be changed.
Don't think you know it all.
Don't think that everyone is like you.
Don't think that people should think like you.
Don't assume that people are good.
Don't assume that science is proved.
Don't presume a finite realm.

What is right today as history has shown, it is a best guess in
the realm of the unknown.
So, don't be surprised if you were wrong.

Understanding

I understand
I see, I know, I capitulate
Knowing
Knowing what?
Knowing a fact.
Is your knowing Objective or Subjective?

Singular understanding.
You perceive something to be fact.
This is your singular subjective observation.

Plural understanding.
You and others agree on a fact.
Is that then Objective?
We understand?

I see the man is dead.
We see the man is dead.
Therefore, the man must be dead.

But,
I love.
You say you love.
I cannot feel what you feel.
Therefore, I doubt.
I only know that I love,
And your love must be proved.

A God in heaven alone is the God of nothing.

Eternal

A young confidant said to me, "I find the idea of everlasting life absurd in that he would be bored with everything being the same and there would be nothing more to do." I responded, "Interesting, perhaps ignorance is then bliss, that continuance is best served by the newborn, yet unfettered mind; for if you continue too long you are not impressed with the value of your existence?"

He said, "Logically, if all things were accomplished, he would rather not be than to continue in eternal monotony." I responded, "Thus is the error of finite thinking that resolves itself to conclusion that eternal life has limitations."

And now a consideration of relativity as in Einstein's consideration of time, absolute zero is impossible. This means that for all eternity to pass in zero time would equate to non-existence, thus eternity is just that, "eternal." The progression through time is relative to the observer's velocity, but velocity relative to what?

Consider Descartes' existential proof, "I am thinking, therefore I am." Extended in an objective consideration, "We are thinking; therefore, we are." Thus, non-existence is disproved, albeit only temporally over the course of recorded history.

Duration or time is only relative to memory, and everlasting life only has meaning if finite life is remembered and thus the differential. You could not know the eternal unless you first know the finite; or rather you must die to live. It can be no other way.

To assume that you understand and have conclusion in your finite realm and thinking only shows your simple limitations.

The Rambling of the wayward Mind

Caught with relief on a cool morning after a long stretch of
summer heat,
as the clouds shroud the morning sun,
I'm beset with contemplations of the labor of the day before.

The world around is buzzing with busyness as each individual
chases the necessary needs of survival, of want, of pleasure.

This amounts to labor for the most of us, with the manipulation
by the cunning, which are the least of us, that conspire to avoid
life's labor. But always is the constant churning of ambition.

Imagine an iron anchor for a sailing vessel attached to an
unbreakable chain.
Now, cast it overboard, hard upon the rocks and feel the
wayward ship come to a stop.
Slow the mindless ambition, and rest.

Long life is not hurried.
Be not bored with simplicity and take time to taste and savor.
And the cool breeze washes over me, a breeze I would not have
felt lest I stop to feel it.

Happiness

I came upon a couple of young cohorts of the zeitgeist mentality.

They were embroiled in a heated conversation of their frustration with their material situation. Basically, they felt outside of the wealth and prosperity they see around them and were assured that the design of society was to keep them from reaching the brass ring and they themselves from being rich.

I listened knowing that at this point in the conversation I could not get the 'proverbial word' in edgewise. I made a little squeaking sound and they said, "What is that?" I said the cliché, "It is a word trying to get in edgewise."

I then said, "What is Happiness," and I reminded them of the 'Declaration of Independence' which states the equality of men and the right to the pursuit of happiness. I then ask them to define happiness.

They pondered for a moment as I goaded them with my favorite spiel which is as I stated first rapidly, "Love, Hate, Joy, Grief, Fear, Jealousy and Grace." They said, "What?" So, I repeated, "Love, Hate, Joy, Grief, Fear, Jealousy and Grace," and I iterated, "I'm happy when I love, have Joy and Grace and I'm dismayed when I hate have grief or fear or jealousy.

And I continued which is hard to do when a sage is trying to get into the minds of the young. I said, "Let's start with jealousy." I started with jealousy because that is what I could hear so pronounced in their conversation." I said, "The primary needs of the human animal are, food, shelter and clothing." This is grade school social studies education which is often overlooked because it is not really put into context.

I continued with Socratic dialog, "Do you have Food?" They said, "Yes but cheap stuff not that of the rich, like expensive steak and lobster." To which I rolled my eyes and admonished them to continue to listen. I said, "Do you have shelter?" One of them still lived at home with his parents and the other had an apartment. The one with the apartment acknowledge that he had a crummy little apartment. I continued with, "And, you both look like you have clothes and are quite well dressed." They agreed.

I said, "So you have all of the basic necessities which if you did not have these I would account that with unhappiness. But since you have these, I should say you are happy that you are not poor." Of course, this did not please them.

They started in with a malaise of the 'oppression by the rich' and 'their long hours and low pay' and again I made a squeaking sound trying to break in, "Let me continue." It is hard to get them to stop the speech center in the brain that flows endlessly.

Now I did a little inventory of their possessions again with Socratic questioning and discovered for them their many things which in this day are so common. They had cars and televisions and stereos and cell phones and video games. They bought fast food and power drinks and spent money at entertainment clubs but considered themselves oppressed by the rich and they were wonton.

Again, fighting to get them to listen, I raised my voice, "Do all those things you have bring you Joy?" They mumbled, "Sort of, but those are just toys; it is not what we really want."

I seized on the moment, "What is it you really want; what is it that will really make you happy." They went on with a list of bigger and better stuff and of course higher pay."

I had them where I wanted them, "You have graduated from school and you have read history and the struggles of the past, but you learned nothing, and if you do not place yourself into history and struggle, you will never understand and for this reason I will place you as spoiled, jealous children pampered with toys and this is no one's doing but your own with one exception…, The world teaches you megalomania.

They said, "What?" I said, "You are a 'nobody' unless you are a 'somebody' and you are jealous and filled with hate and grief and rather than saving your money and educating yourself you spend it all on toys and frivolous times and you do nothing productive to enhance your position, if even that, in some way, will make you happy. You are beset with competition and struggle to grasp the proverbial 'Brass Ring' and if you got it, would you then be happy?"

I stated again, "Love, Hate, Joy, Grief, Fear, Jealousy and Grace. You are filled with, Hate, Grief and Fear. You hate your so-called oppression; you are jealous over the possessions of others and you fear you will never have what they have. As a result, you miss out on Love and Joy and Grace which you can find everyday if you would so choose."

I added, "History is wasted on you and as of yet you have learned nothing."

They started in on me, "What about you, you seem to have the so-called toys that we have, are you not the same as us?" To which I said, "No, I, not like you, have happiness. I savor what you may call my mediocre existence and account myself rich compared to poverty and with my age and experience, I have won and lost and won again, which you my young friends will do also and thus is the beauty of the differential."

To this again they said, "What?"

I said, "You can tell a child that the frying pan is hot and to not touch it, but until the child is burned it will not know. I cannot give you happiness, you must find it yourself. I cannot make you feel the suffering of others or have you put on the mantle of that which is taught by history. Blessed is the child that upon hearing the teachings of the father do his instruction without being burned. I only hope for you that I have pointed the way."

And there was silence.

Collection of Love Sonnets

Your Face

Little does the wayward mind know the rambling of its heart.
The feelings of the things unsaid are the most important part.

You wander out to search and find someone to know your soul.
Blinded by the many years despair doth take its toll.

You gaze upon and rarely see what language cannot describe.
A myriad of those forlorn with wants and needs they hide.

There is the unspoken expression, from your soul it does exude.
You carry it always with you; for most it does elude.

Some may call it an aura that encases the thing within.
So listen now my darling for this tale I will begin.

Many years have passed me by in search for one to know.
The love I have inside me that oft times brings me low.

I've seen so many faces and lovely ones for sure.
Such beauty can delude one with sickness and no cure.

You walk amongst the beauty and gaze deep into their eyes.
Yet something leaves you empty understanding beauties lies.

Wander here and wander there and thus the wayward mind.
Would be better if I never gazed and God should strike me
blind.

I've seen so many faces and lovely to be sure.
There seems to be no comfort for my sickness not a cure.

Does not beauty know this, that pretentiousness is seen?
It's a telling aura and the truth we easily can glean

The face is the extruding spirit of the soul that lies within.
It harbors all the telling from forehead to the chin.

The eyes are most expressive for they do say quite a lot.
They tell all things about you whether willing or whether not.

So, hearken to this traveler whose search was too and fro.
I've seen so many faces all leaving me so low.

I'm looking for that one face I really want to know.
No question of my journey for on it I must go.

Travel here travel there subconscious is my distain.
I avoid being callous with endurance I do maintain.

Years pass with vanity's toll alone to say it best.
I see couples good and bad while lonely are the rest.

You never know the day or hour when fate will come your way.
Could it be in the evening or a bright and sunny day?

But it happened. What happened? It. It happened. Again, what
happened?

I saw your face; I saw this most amazing face. It was so telling.

No pretentiousness, nothing hid; nothing to hide.

So aback was I taken that I had to gaze from afar.

I had to grip my feeble mind my thinking was ajar.

I don't believe I've found this beauty so demure.
I have to be so cautious my confidence so unsure.

I want this stunning beauty to have her for my own.
For forever is my longing or else I die alone.

I've written this before we've met with hope it will come true.

If I never have you, I'll burn this through and through.

I'm captured by your beautiful face and soul that lies within.

With eyes that shine of more than grace to forgive my mortal
sin.

And my sin is wantonness; Wanton of your abiding soul and
your stunning face.

I love you already even from afar.

Every day is the same

Every day is the same to me and that is a good thing not bad.

It is just that I have to deal with it this lovely labor.

Labor as in giving birth or as with a straining back early in the day, for a job you love and want done.

It is something I have to deal with this lovely labor.

Would that it should go away I would want to have it back; this labor, this lovely labor.

For you see I labor to understand why a woman as beautiful as you loves a man like me and I pray you will never stop, for surely, I will weep to have that labor back or die in vain.

Think Lovely

Think Lovely;
pink roses, hummingbirds, autumn colors and rainbows.
Think Joy;
laughing children, kind smiles, sweet hello's and lovers.
Think comfort;
downy beds, cool in summer, warm in winter and hugs.
Think beautiful;
mountain streams, golden sunsets, the fairest of maidens and
you.

Loves Rare Scene

Morning broke and for a moment the sun shone through a sever in the clouds;
Nestled in a cabin in the forest, in the wood, we are far from cares and concerns.

The sever closes and the red gleam of the sun dims as more soft clouds envelope us.
You come to me with warm drink and pastry as an ever so gentle rain begins.

It is warm yet cool because of the rain, this lovely soft rain that soothes the mind.
And, then the music begins, that lovely cherished sound that is only your voice.

It is the voice of my love, my darling one that so graces me with her presence and love.
At times I fear the loss of my own soul if she should be gone.

And then you take me with your cunning and comfort, body to body beyond measure.
Nature in the midst of nature and you love me beyond measure, body to body and body to soul. The animals watched with no concern as if to learn from this rare scene.

And the lovely rain came down and ecstasy was known.

I do so love you.

I Dreamt a Little Heaven

I arose from my sleep and sat to gaze upon you as you lay.
I had to rub my eyes, astonished at what I saw.

You lay there so beautiful and calm with a breath that is so
sweet.
Beside you were four tiny angles about a quarter of your size.

Nestled against you on both sides were sleeping angles.
They breathed when you breathed as if connected to you.

I came lucidly to my senses and realized I was dreaming.
Consciousness comes in and I truly wake and reality surrounds
me.

You truly are resting sweetly beside me and the angles are
gone.
I gaze upon you and realize and interpret the dream.

You are just as the angles that I saw beside you, and the
adoration and longing I have for you my love is complete and
true.

And I watched you sleep and I am so much in love.

The Single Woman

I see truth in her eyes through which I can see her soul
Long serving
Hides her pain
Clings to hope
Beams with grace
Gives her most
Cries alone
Wants to share
Longs to understand
Feels forlorn
Prays to God
Sustains with faith
Dulls her pain with drink
She waits and hopes
She dreams of that one shoulder to cry on;
That one who understands.

Have You Ever?

Have you ever known sincerity?
Have you ever known this calm?
Have you ever held a thing of rarity?
Have you ever sung this psalm?

Have you ever danced this dance of joy?"
Have you ever played this tune so rare?"
Have you ever returned to a children's toy"?
Have you ever played without a care?"

Have you ever seen the mockingbird?"
Have you ever known its laughing tease?"
Have you ever heard that loving word?"
Have you ever been so pleased?"

I have for in your eyes is truth'
and you say you love me.

Longing

Tell the birds to stop their singing.
Tell the butterflies to go away.
Tell the bells to stop their ringing
Tell the colors to turn to gray.

Have the clocks to stop their ticking.
Have the children stop their play.
Have the harpist stop her picking.
Have the moon to go away.

Stop the river from its flowing.
Stop the stars and crystal sky.
Stop the breezes from their blowing.
Stop all wonders by and by.

Count the minutes I am mourning.
Count the tear drops from my eyes.
Count the depth of this fore longing.
Count the anguish where it lies.

Please the minstrel to stop playing.
Please the singers to go away.
Please the dancers stop their dancing
Please the pain to stop I pray.

All if this because I miss you.

Contemplations

Aphorism of Agape

Greek has four words for love...

Storge – affection

Philia – friendship

Eros – passionate/sexual

Agape – brotherly/parental also denoted as true love.

All of these types of love except Eros require no reciprocation i.e. you give love because you want to, while expecting nothing in return. Eros is selfish. Eros needs. Eros wants.

Eros is a lie, lose it. I love the Hibiscus flower; it has no capacity to love me in return.

Great expectations of love suffer only the searcher in vain and when discovered, my fickle nature, I loved only the idea of you loving me. I shroud this in a drape of images in my mind, your lovely face, your statures casual lean, your distinctive voice and your unique demeanor. I have this all wrapped up in a neat little package which are all the things I love about you. It was subtle and cautious as we tip toed into love, both willing and wanton to hear those words come from the lips. I love you.

And now that you have fallen into my lovers trap, I expect you to be the person I have imaged you to be. Familiar, unchanging and sure to respond with the words, I love you, when I beckon with the words of the same. And on the day that you don't respond to my call for a love assured, I don't love you, I don't want you, I don't need you, anymore. Because, short of your adorable aura, it was me loving me through the eyes of you, and like the true narcissists we are, you were only in the way of my greatest love which is me.

Now when you are done abusing yourself searching for that one true love, give yourself the greatest gift of agape; that of brotherly love. You love someone just because you love them with nothing in return. All else is wanton and lustful and vain and truly the God Eros is teasing you to fail at the price of your foolish heart. And when you catch them or you are caught, the lust will be done and then what love do you have, but none.

Where Love is made

For this is where love is made.

For I have tried my children in the fire of infirmity; in the incomprehensible pain of the flesh.

They are left alone in the dark without guidance or light to see.
I must at my own anguish leave them alone to see, to see if they are of mine own sinew.

If they are of mine own, if they are of mine heart, they will surely, truly be kindred.

Love cannot be demanded only offered and it is only seen through longing.

In the midst of love it is squandered and taken for granted and thus it is only seen when lost.

For in the differential of having and not having is the realization and true definition that gives love its deepest meaning.

Thus, the reason for the universe and all existence is love and a God who incomprehensibly demanded it and went away in anguish for this tyrannical demand.

There can be no other way. You must lose to gain. You must die to live.

And, a God in heaven alone is the God of nothing.

You think this is without design, that all of existence just happened?

Look deep and you will see your want; your want to be, your want to go somewhere, your want to do something, your want rise above this earthly, fleshly, limited realm.

You want.

You want to reach someone, to tell someone, to hear someone, to be recognized by someone and to recognize someone.

And a God in heaven alone is the God of nothing.

While the frustration of your limited time, and your frustration with your limited ability and your frustration with others ability to understand your frustration, your reaching, your longing to do and accomplish and to aid and comfort and fix the ills of all is so sorrowfully misunderstood.

So, this is where love is made, when you are dried up and all you strength is gone in your anguish to demand love. You came with all your heart to do that spirit that is in you, that thing that you are, this soul, this entity, which is you, which is how you were made.

In the image of God were you made, that of Love, Hate, Joy, Grief, Fear, Jealousy and Grace and you are swimming in the void, in darkness hoping and thus you are kindred. For you are kindred and like God knowing Gods want.

For a God in heaven alone is the God of nothing.

For this realm is truly designed. It is designed to find the lonely, the broken and the wanton heart that will cherish life even at the cost of its own, lest forever you are alone, lest forever you be alone.

And, love was nailed to a tree, not the tree of good and evil but of life.

Ignorance vs. Stupidity

In no manner should one be so cruel as to hold one accountable for not knowing a priori in this incredibly complex existence.

I contend that darkness requires no creation but is only revealed by the virtue of the light; that light is and darkness is the lack of light.

Likewise, even God cannot be held accountable for the creation of darkness. This would hold also that ignorance requires no creation and that any sentient being that comes into existence from a previous state of nonexistence is incapable of knowing a priori. Thus, God is not responsible for the creation of ignorance; that it requires no creation and exists a priori; however, it is logically possible for one to know that ignorance is an existential condition of all new entrants to this realm. We know a priori that our children are empty vessels with the exception of basic instincts and wants. They are ignorant through no fault of their own or Gods.

One might consider that we are in a continual condition of ignorance until time unfolds in the present to reveal the day's teachings and in past tense only can we say we understand.

Memory, if it serves us well guides us through a maze of decisions on a daily basis that as we mature, we do not make the same mistake twice. If we do make a mistake twice, one then chastises oneself and we might respond as our inner voice states, "How stupid I was. I already knew this," as we then correct our mistake a second time vowing that it will never happen again."

Thus, we released the worse condemnation we could upon ourselves which to use the word 'stupid.'

If one is a kind person, one would never use this term on anyone but one's self and interestingly enough we generally use it on ourselves quite often and if you don't perhaps you should. I digress.

By dictionary definition stupid is ... "having or showing a great lack of intelligence or common sense." I use a quip at times in an attempt to be humorous, it is that the definition of stupid is, "one that could learn but refuses."

So, we now come to the purpose of this soliloquy. It is in consideration of the cliché "Crazy stupid love."

It seems to me that the one thing that human beings take so long to learn and stupidly will return to where they have failed time and time again is the trough of romantic love. One wishes to drink even though they having been to the trough before had only found it empty or even the water poison.
Now youthful ignorance is excusable as youthful ignorance and thus it gets a pass perhaps several times. As statistics would show those persons in matrimonies that last is approximately fifty percent of the total population. If one assumes that matrimonies that last equate to love's success then we are left to the other fifty percent that are mysterious wanderers or searchers or lost vagabonds on the sea of love.
There is perhaps a percentage that feels they have come to the logical understanding that romantic love is a contrivance and in fact does not exist.

These I would contend are the ones that through ignorance and stumbling actually learned something and can free themselves from the definition of stupid.

I would contend that romantic love is like casting your fate to the wind, it is something ignorant children do with bliss. The heart of a sage hardened by failure learns…

One loves a flower because it is beautiful not because the flower loves them in return.
One does not love by choice nor is one loved by demand.
You love just because you love and if you are loved in return rejoice.

So therefore, I am not stupid.
That is until the next time.

An Existential Portrayal of the Spirit
(In Other Words – Ideology)

Define the world as mineral, animal and spirit.
Mineral such as solid, liquid and gas.
Animal such as animated mechanical mineral.
Spirit, as in a metaphysical manipulation of the mineral.

Amino acidic protein formation animated the base forms of
matter.
Solid, liquid and gas in an amorphous reaction of differentials
of
Light and dark, hard and soft, hot and cold,
differentiated into a stratum.
Now this is an existential observation that can be translated -
into a spectrum.

The differential by analysis is mysterious.
The spectrum of elements is periodic but broken with elements
that should be but are not.
These are found as elements that can be created but whose life
span is periodically short.

Belay the mechanical consideration in lust for the metaphysical.

Imbued in the human experience is the spirit that motivates the
mineral.
This animated mineral, amino acidic protein, differentiated into
an evolved organism over eons of time. This highly evolved
chemical machine speaks and has the capability to manipulate,
not only its mineral form but also the other mineral and animal
forms within its realm.

So thus, you have animals such as humans that walk and talk and express ideas to influence and/or manipulate other mineral forms.

Curious enough is the amazement that mineral became animated, but that the result presented a metaphysical consciousness which looked back upon itself with observation.

"I am thinking therefore I am."

One must consider that ideas are but vapor upon the wind. Mineral speaks and records on paper and now other media its spirit or rather ideas.

If you erase the paper or memory, the ideas or ideology are lost. Without remembrance or documentation by whatever media, the mindset or ideology is lost.

Existential observation indicates that the instinct for survival exists in all species.
Pure and simple is the mineral/animal's fight for life and with fierce carnality it fights to live.

"To be or not to be?"

Is this the spirit?

Consider the metaphysical manifestation of the will of the mineral?
Cast into space upon the wind, by screech and cry, by scream and whimper, on breath of air and by word.

The Differential

Light is. Darkness is the lack of light.

Hard is. Softness is the lack of hardness
Heat is, cold is the lack of heat.

Metaphysical Differential is not tangible.
It exists only by virtue of the spoken word.
Like vapor on the wind it is delicate and temporal.

Stated
Love vs. Hate
Joy vs. Grief
Right vs. Wrong
Justice vs. Injustice
Good vs. Bad
or rather
Good vs. Evil

These differentials do not exist physically they only exist
metaphysically.
And in the scope of epochs of time it could evaporate in one
simple
cataclysmic event that reduces the human race to dust.

The question is - like spring from the death of winter and
seed germinating from the ashes of fire,
would the metaphysical ideology or spirit emerge when there is
no physical
documentation or memory to carry it forward.

Since Justice and its concept only exists in the human animal
metaphysically as an idea,
would it again emerge from cataclysm?

Through trials and tribulations and evolution would the concept
of

87

justice again emerge from the abyss like the animated mineral emerged?

We are physical stuff that moves by the virtue of the needs for survival like every animal.

The spirit is a vaporous word transmitted through the air from being to being.
However, it conveys the entity from which it emerges.
Thus, I am the mineral that speaks.
Thus, you are.
And thus, justice and justification for your right to life is defended by you, life and limb.

And the trial of your right to exist is held in the court of the theater of the world,
where your vaporous ideas are tested.

Salutations to Herman Hess

I hope to be laughed out of court.

Cognizance and Kindness

No one told you that the prerequisite to be a human entity was to be judged, but then you must first be made in flesh and bone before you can be asked the question of the prerequisite to your existence is to be judged as to your right to exist at all.

For this God is sorry that you could not be asked if you want to exist prior to your creation. Now for God to be sorry for not asking you a priori is substantial. Such that his condemnation for such responsibility required his own death.

How could one know a priori that one offends unless first the error of offence is experienced and only posteriori can one make amends.

Glory may just be this, that God a priori apologized for your suffering and took upon himself the complete punishment for having created death and judgement and salvation and forgiveness for the creation of an entity which is you, for which God hoped to commune except that forgoing his creation was ignorant.

Omnipotence conceived a realm in which sacrifice, and punishment befell upon itself to pay for all sin and death and judgement. Existence itself is juxtaposed against this differential. How can complete judgement not be tyrannical? How could anyone be free if continually judged? And, if God created man for his own companion, likened unto himself, free and autonomous, how could that be accomplished under continual judgement.

Cognizance.

Unrighteousness is self-incriminating, and unkindness is self-evident. An omnipotent God provided a way around ignorance, it is called forgiveness. You would not punish a child for its ignorance and thus they learn and not fear their parent.

If it is not of kindness, it is not of God.

Eternity Waits

The sun rose today like any other day. But nothing happened. No murder, no death, no tragedy.

What if eternity were days and days where nothing happened?

Could it be that the mundane reality of eternity is nothing but day after day of no events, with the sun rising and setting?

Albeit with glorious color and sweet aroma of flora and salt air, with waves trashing the shore and sunset sweeping to reveal the stars and a full moon rising?

A cool breeze came across the ocean and the smell of the bounty of the sea was enticing and comforting with the aroma of the eternal, yet nothing happened today, no murder, no death, no tragedy in the human realm.

All the earth is subject to the human realm.

But they conceived this day with murder and death and tragedy and the sun rose and set, and the ocean waves churned and eternity waits for fools who could learn but refuse.

Personal note

This is an excerpt from a blog post about a comment.

Rarely do I get curious feedback but then sometimes it comes. "Oh, so welcome, yet it comes."

The question was, "I find that you repeat two statements often in your writings, one is 'the differential' and the other is 'a god in heaven alone is the god of nothing.' " What is your reasoning? Why are you fixated on this?

Thank you, 'anonymous' for your query.

Are we allowed to consider all things? Are we brave enough? Do we have the right?

If you live, you have the right and you are allowed to consider all things. It does not matter whether you are brave enough, because truth is. However, truth can be confused with subjective observation and want.

In physics, the "uncertainty principle" or rather the probability that the observer affects the observation is always a consideration. How can one step outside of ones own realization to be truly objective? The answer is you cannot.

I entertain myself by asking acquaintances at special moments, "What is the meaning of life?" As they ponder, I am prepared with a response. When they say, "I don't know, maybe this or that..."

I respond, "You. You are the meaning of life," and I continue. "You are the observer of life and the only meaning it has is what it means to you. Otherwise it has no meaning. You are the subjective purpose of your life. If the entire universe exists, it is of no matter except that it is rationalized by your entity which is you, and it must be of value to you and your self-consideration. If it should not be about you and your self-consideration then existence, as far as you are concerned it is of no value. Then by your own virtue, you and it (the universe) would cease to exist. The universe does not see you, you see it, but since you are made of the substance of the universe then you must be it, and it must be you.

No proof of your existence is necessary. You are.

One might consider the first law of thermodynamics. Energy can neither be created nor destroyed. It can only change form. The second law is entropy.

Faint of heart, sleep lest you realize you cannot - not be - or rather you cannot un-be. Death will render you to a new state and remember energy can neither be created nor destroyed. Your entity is an energy that cannot be destroyed.

Thus, I now expound on to the first question of my so-called fixation, "the differential"

Nothing can be realized without differentiation. If all matter was homogenous the universe would be at a complete entropic state. No particles would collide or touch each other and no existence could be realized. No heat, no cold, no light nor darkness by virtue of light, no hard, no soft, no pressure or vacuum which is a lesser pressure. There would be no differentiation; there would be no possibility of space or time.

Now consider... Rather than belaboring the causality of our existence and origin such as the "Big Band," we by experiment, portend to accept that we and the universe exist and as a truly existential objective observation, the universe and existence itself, is the definition of the eternal and infinite. That by its (the universe) very nature and (us) made of the substance of the universe are anything other than infinite and eternal. That is to say, the existential nature of infinity and eternity is in itself us. The oddity and impossibility is infinite entropy and no differentiation.

If you disagree, I would contend that you do not have a grasp of infinity or eternity or probability over infinite time. It in itself allows for infinite dimensions and possibilities of existential realms.

The only consideration becomes one of physical scientific proof. Thus, is my dedication to the differential as a concept. It is by differentiation that we perceive all things, be it physical or metaphysical. It is by this manner that I have juxtaposed the underlying psychological motivations of the human animal.

When I reiterate the expression, Love, Hate, Joy, Grief, Fear, Jealousy and Grace, these are differentials which appear in us all as causality for why we do what we do in social interaction.

As to my quip, "A God in Heaven Alone is the God of Nothing"

Having been a biblical researcher and self-professed theologian, I approach God as a child would his father. To explain... a child has no fear of its father, if its father loved and cherished the child. Since my experience as a child imbued in me my father's love, I ask anything without fear or reprisal even of the proverbial God. Searching human nature and my very soul I came to a conclusion. I only exist because of you and without you, I am sad and sorrowful and miserably alone. I need you to be, I need you to be so that I'm not alone. In this I contend that again because of differentiation the state of loneliness and separation is juxtaposed to love, acceptance and joy. Even if there are times when you cast me out and force your hate on me such that I should hate you, I know the depths of eternal loneliness, when you find yourself a vagabond such that all despise you, and to this I say I want death and separation from my anguish that I should be alone, eternally alone weeping that I have failed to find anyone kindred. I contend that the most sorrowful state is to be unappreciated and unloved, and I contend that this is the soul of you and the manner in which you were made. And if this is not the manner in which you were made then it is not of God for the greatest failure of God would be to be unloved and thus, I say, "For a God in Heaven Alone is the God of nothing."

Search your soul for this biblically is "the image with which you were made," one of Love, Hate, Joy, Grief, Fear, Jealousy and Grace, the seven spirits of God spoken of in the book of Revelation. You are set in tribulation in this realm by reason, by necessity for differentiation and separation to find your very nature. This is a trial, a forging, a test for a just and tyrannical demand, the demand of love. For the final state of your quantum mechanical existence is the realization that you cannot cease to be and to your great joy or eternal shame, you are what you are, good or evil.

And the final state…

Love, Joy and Grace and infinites' challenge, which is that of boundless creation and invention. Think not? Then your feeble mind has decided all infinity resolved to your own understanding and the differential to your thinking is zero which is impossible because zero does not exist.

Many Regards

T J Ginn

Made in the USA
Columbia, SC
11 November 2024

45931911R00054